IT'S A CHILD'S WORLD

Pollution, Recycling, Trash, and Litter

Using Nonfiction to Promote Literacy Across the Curriculum

by Doris Roettger

Fearon Teacher Aids
Simon & Schuster Supplementary Education Group

Teacher Reviewers

Rebecca Busch
San Antonio, Texas

Nora Forester
San Antonio, Texas

Delphine Hetes
Detroit, Michigan

Debbie Kellogg
West Des Moines, Iowa

Editorial Director: Virginia L. Murphy

Editor: Virginia Massey Bell

Copyeditor: Susan J. Kling

Illustration: Anita Nelson

Design: Terry McGrath

Cover Design: Lucyna Green

ISBN 0-86653-981-6

Printed in the United States of America

1. 9 8 7 6 5 4 3

A Note from the Author

Children have a natural curiosity about the world in which they live. They are intensely interested in learning about real things, real places, and real people. They also enjoy and learn from hands-on experiences. Nonfiction books and magazines provide opportunities for children to explore their many interests and extend their base of knowledge.

Reading nonfiction materials is different from reading picture or storybooks. To be effective readers, children need to learn how to locate the information or find answers to their many questions. They also need to learn to think about and evaluate the accuracy of any information presented. Finally, they need opportunities to learn the relationship between what they read and the activities in which they apply their new knowledge.

You, as the teacher, can provide opportunities for children to learn from their observations, their reading, and their writing in an integrated language-arts approach across the curriculum.

Modeling thinking strategies and then providing practice across the curriculum will help students become observers and explorers of their world, plus effective users of literacy skills. Encouraging children to extend and demonstrate their understanding through a variety of communication areas—speaking, reading, drama, writing, listening, and art—is also very valuable.

The suggestions in this guide are action-oriented and designed to involve students in the thinking process. The activities do not relate to any one single book. Instead, the strategies and activities are designed to be used with any of the books suggested in the bibliography or with books found in your own media center. The suggested interdisciplinary activities can also be used across grade levels.

Each lesson begins with the reading of a nonfiction book, book chapter, or magazine article—any title that relates to the follow-up activities. During the activity phase and at other class times, students are encouraged to return to the nonfiction selections available in the classroom to find answers to their questions, compare and verify their observations, and add any new information to their current knowledge base.

The individual theme units are designed to be used for any length of time—from a few days to a month or more, depending on the needs and interests of your students.

Suggested goals for this unit are provided near the beginning of this guide on page 16. The webs on pages 7–9 give you an overview of the areas in which activities are provided.

On each page of this guide, there is space for you to write reflective notes as well as ideas that you want to remember for future teaching. This guide is designed to be a resource from which you make the decisions and then select the learning experiences that will be most appropriate for your students.

Doris Roettger

Contents

Literacy Skills

The following literacy skills are addressed in the *Pollution, Recycling, Trash, and Litter* theme guide.

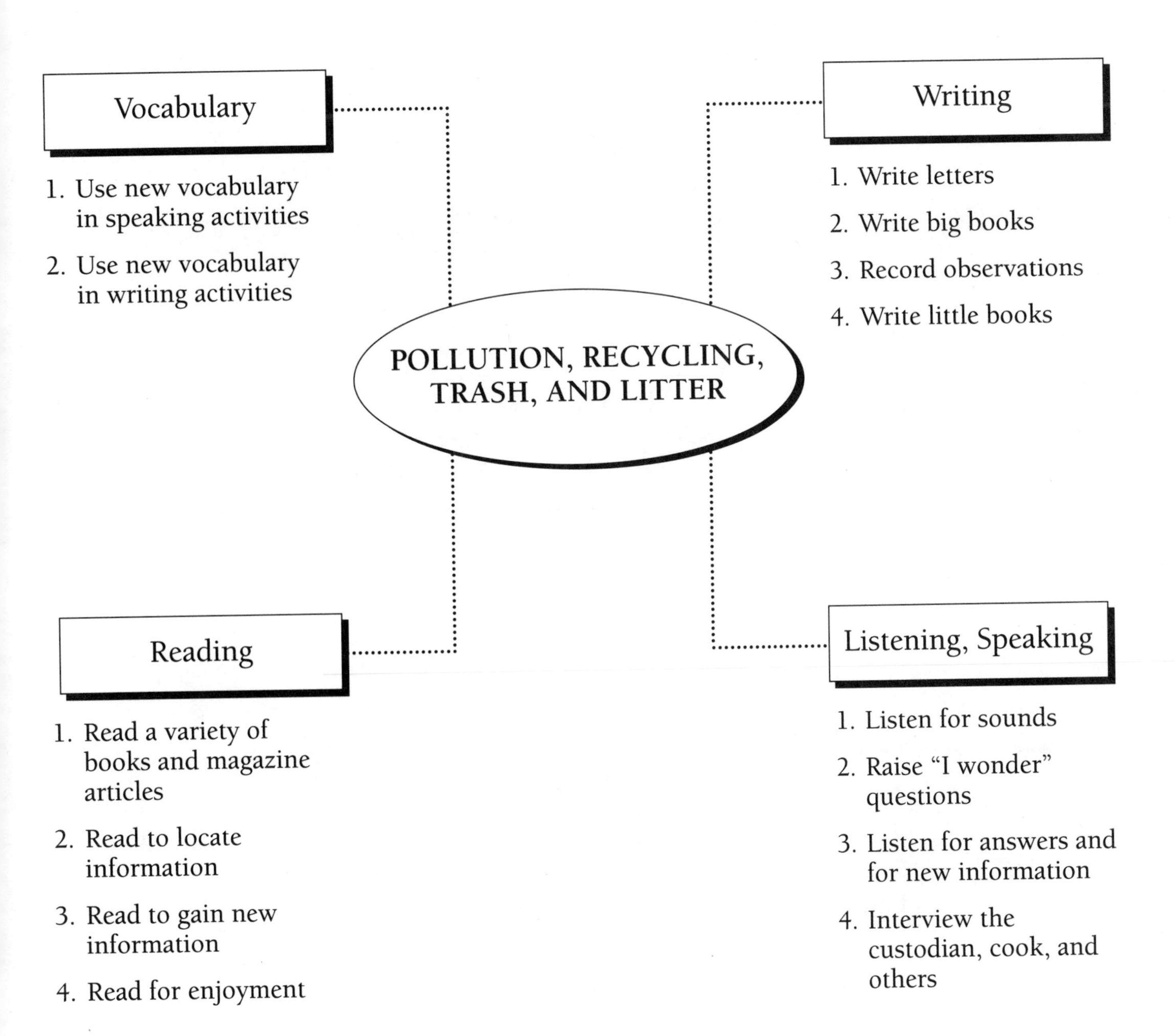

Interdisciplinary Skills

The following interdisciplinary skills are addressed in the *Pollution, Recycling, Trash, and Litter* theme guide.

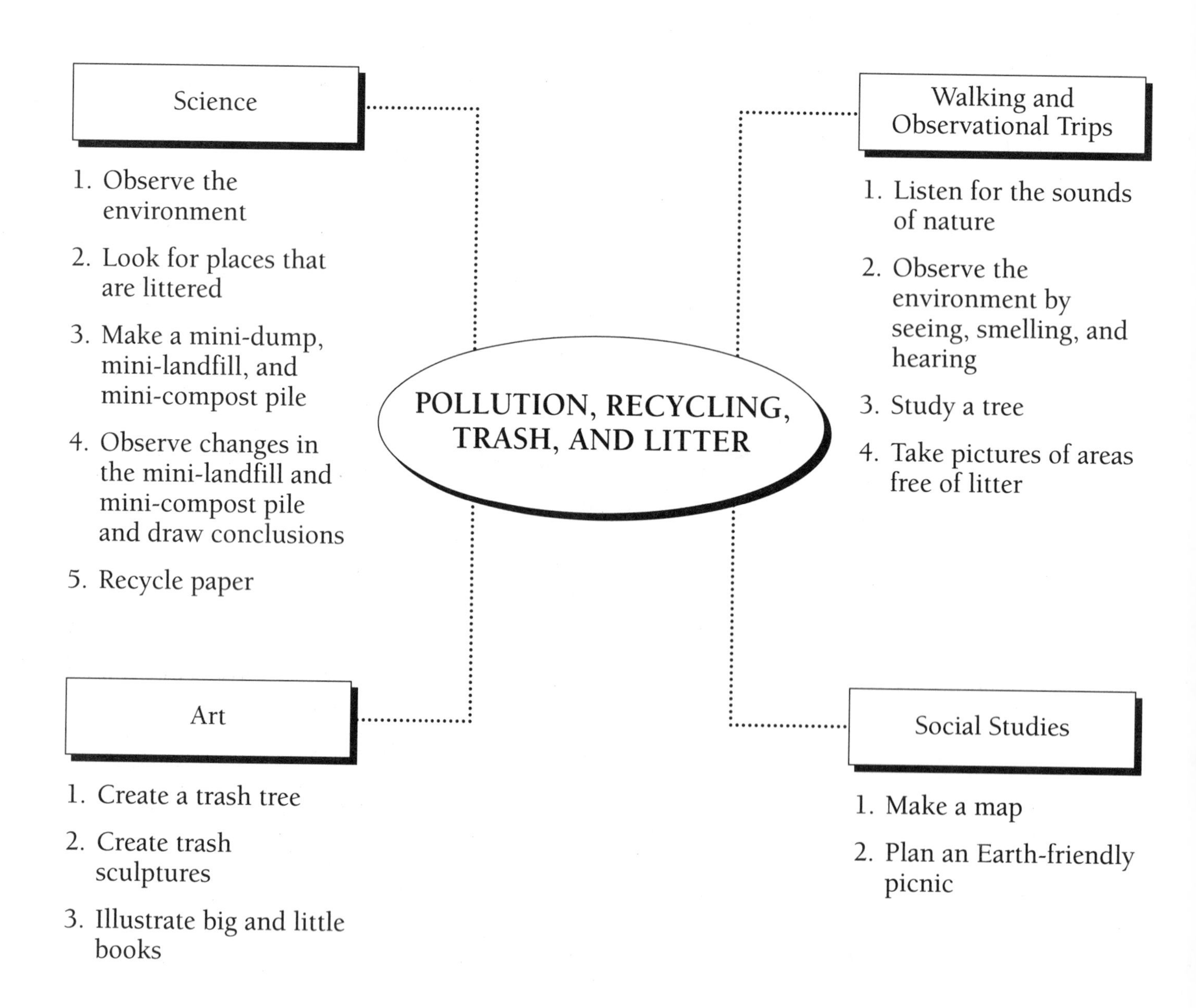

Learning and Working Strategies

The following learning and working strategies are addressed in the *Pollution, Recycling, Trash, and Litter* theme guide.

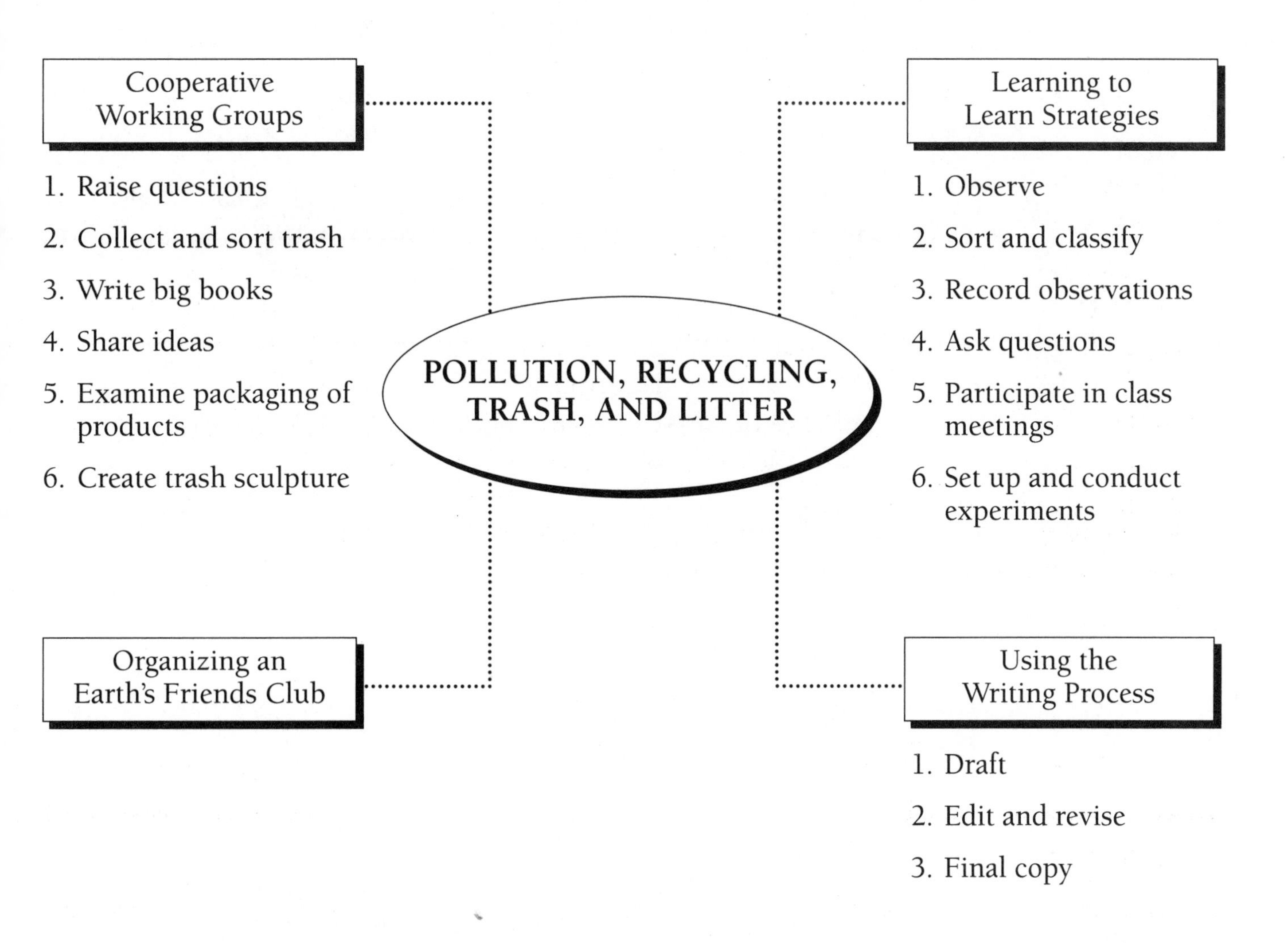

About Pollution, Recycling, Trash, and Litter

Protecting the environment is a significant concern of many people today—both adults and children. In this unit, children learn how to appreciate the environment and help protect our precious natural resources. Below are a few definitions and statistics that may be helpful to you as you teach this unit.

The term *garbage* refers mainly to food waste, while *rubbish* consists of materials that will not decay, such as plastics, paper, bottles, and tin cans. *Compost* is shredded garbage, leaves, and manure exposed to heat, oxygen, and moisture and is eventually used for fertilizer. A *sanitary landfill* is a sealed area where solid wastes are buried and the ground water is monitored for seepage of dangerous chemicals. A *dump* (currently discouraged in most areas) is where solid waste is simply deposited.

An average family in the United States consumes over 2,000 pounds of paper, approximately 500 pounds of metals, 500 pounds of glass, and 500 pounds of food scraps per year. An average person in the United States produces each year a ton of solid waste.

The composition of solid waste produced by an average community consists of 50.6% paper, 19.6% food waste, 10.1% glass, 9.9% metal, 3.5% wood, 3.0% textiles, 1.75% leather and rubber, 1.4% plastics, and 0.2% miscellaneous.

There are ways of significantly reducing the amount of waste we produce. Turning sand into glass takes a great deal of energy. Less energy is needed to melt the glass down to make new bottles and jars. Each year, approximately 4 billion trees are cut down to make paper products. Using recycled paper saves hundreds of thousands of trees. Over 80% of general household waste, including food scraps, can be recycled. Solid waste that is burned or incinerated can be reduced by 10 to 15% of its original volume.

There are many products used in this country that cannot be recycled and are deposited in landfills. These products are made from several different materials and cannot be broken down or recycled. For example, aerosol cans (which also contain chemicals that contribute to air pollution) are made from different kinds of metals; juice boxes consist of several layers of material, such as plastic and aluminum foil; and plastic squeeze bottles are made up of different types of plastic.

There are many organizations and publications with additional information for you and your students. Addresses and telephone numbers are available in your library or local directory. Some are listed here for your convenience.

For information on Earth Day, write:

Earth Day
Box AA
Stanford University
Stanford, CA 99305

For information on environmental conservation, call or write:

We Cry Out
Earth Communications Office
314 N. Harper Ave.
Los Angeles, CA 90048
(213) 932-7968

U.S. Environmental Protection Agency
Office of Communications and Public Affairs
401 M St. SW, PM211B
Washington, DC 20460
(202) 382-2080

For information on energy conservation, write or call:

U.S. Department of Energy
Conservation and Renewable Energy Inquiry Referral Service
P.O. Box 8900
Silver Spring, MD 20907
(800) 523-2929

For information on environmental organizations with programs for children, contact:

Sierra Club
730 Polk St.
San Francisco, CA 94109
(415) 776-2211

Suggested Reading Selections

A variety of nonfiction and fiction selections for the primary grades is suggested for use with this theme unit. You will probably want to assemble a collection of materials ahead of time. Or, you may wish to have the students help collect several titles from the library as a group activity. The number and type of selections you and the children read will depend on the length of time you devote to this unit, as well as the availability of titles and the level of your students.

Nonfiction Books

50 Simple Things Kids Can Do to Save the Earth by The EarthWorks Group. Kansas City: Andrews and McMeel, 1990. Explains how specific things in a child's environment are connected to the rest of the world and how using them affects the planet.

Good Planets Are Hard to Find by Roma Dehr and Ronald M. Bazar. Vancouver, B.C.: Earth Beat Press, 1989. An environmental information guide, dictionary, and action book for children and adults.

How the Forest Grew by William Jaspersohn. New York: Greenwillow Books, 1980. Describes a gradual transformation of a farm field to a forest. Has excellent descriptions and use of terminology.

Keepers of the Earth by Michael J. Caduto and Joseph Bruchac. Golden, CO: Fulcrum, Inc., 1989. Native American stories and environmental activities for children. A selection of traditional tales from various Indian tribes, each accompanied by instructions for related activities dealing with aspects of the environment.

Let's Be Nature's Friend by Jack Stokes. New York: Henry Z. Walck, Inc., 1977. Offers suggestions in verse for improving our environment through such activities as recycling glass, helping to pass laws against pollution, and saving energy.

Our Changing World: The Forest by David Bellamy. New York: C. N. Potter, 1988. Describes the co-existence of a variety of plants and animals in their natural forest habitat and their struggle to survive a human-made disaster.

Our Changing World: The River by David Bellamy. New York: Crown Publishers, 1988. Relates how plants and creatures co-exist in a river as they struggle to survive a human-made catastrophe.

Rachel Carson: Pioneer of Ecology by Kathleen V. Kudlinski. New York: Viking Penguin, 1988. The life of pioneer environmentalist and writer, Rachel Carson.

Trash by Charlotte Wilcox. Minneapolis: Carolrhoda Books, Inc., 1988. Examines various methods of garbage disposal with an emphasis on sanitary landfills, but also surveying such alternatives as mass burning and recycling.

A Tree Is Nice by Janice May Udry. New York: Harper & Row, 1956. Describes the usefulness of trees, including shade, swings, leaves, and climbing.

Tree Trunk Traffic by Bianca Lavies. New York: E. P. Dutton, 1989. Text and photographs present the animal life on a 70-year-old maple tree.

Fiction Books

Blue Bug's Beach Party by Virginia Poulet. Chicago: Childrens Press, 1975. Before they can have their beach party, Blue Bug and his friends have to clean the litter off the beach.

Just a Dream by Chris Van Allsburg. Boston: Houghton Mifflin, 1990. When he has a dream about a future Earth devastated by pollution, Walter begins to understand the importance of taking care of the environment.

Little Turtle's Big Adventure by David Harrison. New York: Random House, 1969. The story of little turtle who must move from his peaceful pond when bulldozers fill in his home in order to build houses. Follow the turtle on a difficult journey to find a new habitat.

The Lorax by Dr. Seuss. New York: Random House, 1971. In verse, we look at one man's impact on the environment as he ignores the Lorax's wisdom to save the trees.

Maui-Maui by Stephen Cosgrove. Los Angeles: Price Stern Sloan, Inc., 1978. A story of how to conserve and save our world as taught to a group of imaginary creatures by the whale.

Miss Rumphius by Barbara Cooney. New York: Viking Press, 1982. A story in which one person finds a way to make the world beautiful.

Once There Was a Tree by Natalia Romanova. New York: Dial Books, 1985. This beautifully illustrated book is about a stump that remains after a tree is struck by lightning and felled by a woodsman. Many living creatures use this stump to survive.

Stay Away from the Junkyard by Tricia Tusa. New York: Macmillan, 1988. Theo finds out how to turn junk into beauty when he befriends the junkman and his pig in this adventure story.

Trapper by Stephen Cosgrove. Los Angeles: Price Stern Sloan, Inc., 1982. Imaginary creatures teach the reader that nature can be enjoyed by everyone if we all let it be.

The Warville Wizard by Don Madden. New York: Macmillan, 1986. An old man fights a town of litterbugs by sending each piece of trash back to the person who dropped it.

Poetry

"Tryin' on Clothes" from *A Light in the Attic* by Shel Silverstein. New York: Harper & Row, 1981.

"Nature Is. . ." from *Book of Poetry* by Jack Prelutsky. New York: Random House, 1983.

Magazine Articles

"Earth Day Special: All About Earth Day" from *Ranger Rick*, National Wildlife Federation, April 1990.

"The Inside Story of Clean Air" from *National Geographic World*, National Geographic Society, September 1990.

"Lighthawk: Spotting Polluters from Planes" from *Ranger Rick*, National Wildlife Federation, February 1991.

"Ocean Dumping" from *Ranger Rick*, National Wildlife Federation, September 1990.

"Our Country's Trash: The Mess We're In" from *Ranger Rick*, National Wildlife Federation, September 1990.

"Rescuing Pelicans" from *Ranger Rick*, National Wildlife Federation, September 1990.

"What Do the Wrights Do Wrong" from *Ranger Rick*, National Wildlife Federation, April 1990.

Teacher Reference

Going Green by John Elkington, Julia Hailes, Douglas Hill, and Joel Makover. New York: Viking Penguin, 1990. A child's handbook to saving the planet. Explains the greenhouse effect and ways to recycle at home and at school.

Worms Eat My Garbage by Mary Appelhof. Kalamazoo, MI: Flower Press, 1982. Explains how to set up and maintain a worm composting system. Includes a glossary.

Instructional Goals

Instructional goals for this theme unit are provided here. Space is also provided so that you may fill in your own individual goals where appropriate as well. By the end of this theme unit, students should be able to:

1. Raise questions about pollution, trash, litter, and recycling based on their own curiosity.
2. Explain why litter is harmful.
3. Know how trash is disposed of in their community.
4. Explain how landfills and compost piles are made.
5. Explain the disadvantages of dumps and landfills and the advantages of compost piles.
6. Describe ways of reducing trash and litter.
7. Describe the importance of recycling.
8. Sort and classify information.
9. Share what they have learned with others.
10. Write about their observations.
11. Use new vocabulary in their speaking and writing.
12. Share what they have learned through writing, art, and drama.
13. ....
14. ....
15. ....
16. ....
17. ....
18. ....
19. ....
20. ....

Getting Started

Developing an Appreciation of Nature and the Environment

The following activities are designed to help launch the *Pollution, Recycling, Trash, and Litter* theme unit. You may want to use all of the activities or only one or two, depending on the needs of your students. At the beginning of each lesson, reading a nonfiction book or magazine selection to the class serves as a motivator and helps students become more familiar with and involved in using nonfiction selections. You'll also want to provide plenty of opportunities for children to return to nonfiction selections independently during the activity phases and at other times during class periods as well.

NOTES

1. Vocabulary

a. Create a wall mural of new vocabulary words. As you go through this unit, add any new words the children encounter. Write each new word on a card. Write the word's definition on a second card. Have the children paint a two-sided mural of grass and sky. Add the word cards to one side of the mural and the definition cards to the other.

b. Hang the mural low enough for the children to match words with their definitions. Matching might be accomplished with colored yarn or color-coded clothespins. Post a chart with the correct answers nearby for self-checking.

2. Colors in Nature

Here's an activity that encourages children to take a closer look at their environment. This activity is appropriate for both large groups or smaller groups.

a. Mix paint into colors commonly found outdoors, such as green, brown, black, yellow, or blue. Have a paintbrush available for each color. Place a large sheet of paper on the floor. Paint an abstract shape while everyone counts to three.

b. One child chooses a color and paints while the other students count to three. Each child paints, one at a time, while the others count.

c. After everyone has had an opportunity to paint, ask the children to create interesting designs by blowing on the wet paint and tilting the paper.

d. After the paint is dry, cut up the paper so that everyone receives a piece. Have the children go outside and try to find something in nature that matches the color on their piece of paper. Afterwards, hold a class meeting to discuss what the children found.

NOTES

3. Listening for Sounds in Nature

Take children outside and ask them to close their eyes, be very quiet, and listen for the sounds made in nature, such as birds chirping or leaves rustling. Have the children list every sound they hear. Caution children not to list sounds made by people, such as cars, buses, sirens, or talking. Give children about three minutes to listen. Discuss how many different sounds were heard and what the sounds were. Create a chart of sounds heard by the class.

4. Taking an Outdoor Trip

Plan an outdoor walk in a park to observe the environment and see, hear, and smell the many wonders of nature. A letter to send home explaining the purpose of the trip is provided on page 64. Before taking the children outside, share a brief outline of what they will be doing. Some things you might ask children to look for include:

very tall trees

plants with different-shaped leaves

flowers

moss or weeds

5. Taking Pictures of Areas Free of Litter

Take pictures of places that are attractive and free of litter. This can include trees, shrubs, flower beds, lawns, ponds, or pools. Create a bulletin board of the photos. Encourage children to bring to school pictures of well-kept, attractive areas from newspapers, magazines, or family albums.

6. Studying a Tree

NOTES

Find a tree near the school that the children can observe often.

a. Determine how tall the tree is by comparing its size with the size of nearby buildings. Ask children to notice the shape of the tree as well. Encourage children to make the shape of the tree with their bodies.

b. If possible, pick up some leaves from off the ground. Ask children to think of words that describe how the leaves feel—smooth or pointy, for example. Discuss how the leaves smell as well.

c. Invite the children to lie down under the tree and gaze up through the branches. Ask children to describe what they see.

d. Have children put their arms around the trunk of the tree. Find out if the arms of one child will go all the way around the tree. If the tree is large, help the children predict how many students' arms will be needed to circle the tree. Then have several students measure the tree with their arms joined together.

7. Organizing an Earth's Friends Club

NOTES

Organize an Earth's Friends Club. As a group, decide what children need to do to join the club and when, where, and how often the club will meet. Discuss whether the club should elect leaders as well. Suggested activities for Earth's Friends Club meetings include:

a. making membership cards (see page 63 for a pattern)

b. picking up litter on the school grounds

c. making posters about reducing litter

d. taking cans, plastic bottles, and newspapers to recycling centers

e. planting a tree

f. cleaning up a littered area

g. planting and taking care of flowers

h. listening to speakers talk about ways to reduce litter and trash

Finding Information in Books and Magazines

For each of the following activities, first select a nonfiction book or magazine and then demonstrate how to find information by thinking aloud and having children work through the process with you. Share what you are doing so that children can learn the thought processes as they learn the strategies. Gradually, ask students to think aloud as they locate answers to their own questions as they read as well.

1. Locating Information

a. Help children find books and magazines that pertain to pollution, recycling, trash, or litter.

b. For more advanced readers, model ways children can use a table of contents. Think aloud so students know what you are doing. Then give groups practice identifying titles, page numbers, and locating the pages in books and magazines. Have children think aloud so you know that they understand the process. Repeat the process using an index.

NOTES

2. Finding Answers to Questions

Demonstrate how students can find answers to questions by modeling how you would locate an answer to a question posed by one of the children. Again, think aloud as you find the answer. Give students practice in finding an answer to a question. Ask them to think aloud as they find their answers.

3. Reading for New and Interesting Facts

a. Encourage students to read books of their choice or have older students read several books to a cooperative working group. You might also make tapes of appropriate selections to place in a listening center. Encourage children to watch or listen for new and interesting facts as well as for answers to their questions.

b. Read aloud to the students selections from a number of books suggested in the bibliography. After reading each selection, have children recall the new information they have learned. Record their responses in a web format.

c. Students might also record their questions and answers on Earth shapes. Encourage students to record new and interesting facts they discover in their searches, too.

Real-Life Laboratory

Becoming Aware of Trash and Litter

The activities in this section will heighten children's awareness of litter and trash in the environment. Select one or two books or articles on trash or litter to share with the class before students begin an activity.

1. Taking a Trash Trip

Take students on a walking trip around the school or neighborhood to pick up trash. You will need a trash bag and several pairs of gloves for the children to wear. Plan several trips with the students. Each time you return to class, weigh and chart the trash collected. Note: Be sure there is an adult along with you to supervise what the children pick up and later chart and weigh in class.

THE WEIGHT OF TRASH COLLECTED

Item	Weight	Date

NOTES

2. Sorting and Classifying Trash and Litter

NOTES

Divide the class into cooperative working groups. Take the groups on a trash-collecting trip around the school or neighborhood. After returning to class, have the groups sort the litter and trash they've collected. Ask each group leader to explain why the group members classified the items as they did. Have the groups compare the similarities of their groupings and then chart their findings. Here are some suggestions for classifications:

items that are part of nature

items that are made by people

items that are broken

Items That Are Part of Nature

Items That Are Made by People

Items That Are Broken

Other

NOTES

3. Observing Streets, Yards, and Parks

Ask children to look around the school neighborhood to see if it is free of litter and trash. Take snapshots of any littered areas.

a. Help students make a map of the area around your school. Show the littered areas on the map.

b. Invite the principal, officers of the parent association and, perhaps, community leaders or sanitary officials to come speak to the class. Share the information the class has collected concerning the littered areas. Ask these community leaders to help the class plan a school neighborhood clean-up day.

4. Wall Mural of Words

If you completed the wall mural activity on page 19, you might add the following words and their definitions to the mural at this time:

polluting—making dirty
litter—bits of trash scattered about
trash—material that is thrown away

5. The Classroom Wastebasket

Ask the children to think about how much trash is thrown away each day in just one classroom. Ask the children to weigh the trash in the classroom wastebasket at the end of the day and then sort the trash into categories.

a. Place a large garbage bag in the wastebasket. Near the end of the school day, ask the children to take the bag outside and weigh it. Record the weight of the bag on a chart.

b. Have the children sort the trash inside the bag. As a group, decide on the appropriate categories. Begin a new chart entitled "What's in the Trash in Our Classroom?" Record the information the children discover. Discuss whether everything in the trash actually needed to be thrown away. Could anything have been recycled?

WHAT'S IN THE TRASH IN OUR CLASSROOM?

NOTES

6. The Wastebaskets in Other Classrooms

Ask the children if they would like to weigh and sort the trash from several classrooms to see how much trash is thrown out in one day in the entire school.

a. As a class, write a letter to each classroom asking if the children can pick up each classroom's trash on a designated day.

b. On the day scheduled, have students from the cooperative working groups go to the classrooms to empty the wastebaskets. Weigh each bag and record the weights on a chart.

c. Ask the groups to sort the trash from several classrooms into categories determined by the class. Record the kinds of trash collected. Discuss the findings and share this information with the other classrooms.

7. Finding Out What Happens to the Trash

Invite the school custodian to class to explain what happens to all the trash collected in the classrooms.

8. The Trash at Home

This activity is designed to raise children's awareness of what is thrown away at home. Be sure you get the parents' approval before beginning this activity.

a. Have children bring to school a variety of items that are often thrown away at home. For example,

glass bottles	plastic containers
aluminum cans	paper
egg cartons	Styrofoam trays
aluminum foil	clear plastic wrap
newspapers	grocery bags

b. Hold a class meeting to discuss the uses of each of the items the students bring from home.

c. Suggest that the children survey the garbage in their own homes to see if their family throws away some of the same items. A survey and a letter to send home explaining the purpose of the activity are provided on pages 60 and 61 for your convenience. When the surveys are returned, chart the results.

NOTES

Studying Product Packaging

Over-packaging of products by various industries has become a big concern for environment-conscious citizens. The activities in this section are designed to raise students' awareness of the problem.

1. Examining Packaging

Bring to class a variety of packaging, such as aluminum cans, plastic produce bags, Styrofoam trays from bakery and meat products, and plastic-packaged batteries. Provide time for students in each cooperative working group to examine the different types of packaging. Invite students to bring to class examples of over-packaging from toys and other items, too.

NOTES

2. Raising "I Wonder" Questions

Help students raise "I wonder" questions about packaging. These questions can be written on large sheets of paper and displayed in the classroom. For example,

"I wonder if everything needs to be packaged?"

"I wonder if people would buy batteries if they weren't in a package?"

"I wonder if people would buy meat if it weren't in a Styrofoam package?"

3. Packaging in the School's Cafeteria

Invite the head cook from the cafeteria to come speak to the children about food packaging from the school cook's perspective. Ask him or her to bring some of the packaging to show the class. Discuss what happens to the packaging and whether any of it is recycled or reused.

Dumps, Landfills, and Compost Piles

In this section, students are introduced to the differences between dumps, landfills, and compost piles. They will discover some materials that are biodegradable and some that are harmful to the Earth's environment.

1. Wall Mural of Words

NOTES

If you completed the wall mural activity on page 19, you might add the following words and their definitions to the mural at this time:

sanitary landfill—a sealed area where trash and garbage are buried and the ground water is checked for chemicals that may be leaking

dump—a place where trash and garbage are dumped or deposited without any protection

compost—a mixture of decayed materials and soil that can be used for fertilizer

biodegradable—materials that break down and eventually become part of the soil

2. Raising "I Wonder" Questions

Help children raise "I wonder" questions about what happens to trash, landfills, and so on. These questions can be written on large sheets of paper and displayed in the classroom. For example,

"I wonder what happens to trash that is thrown on the ground?"

"I wonder what happens to items that are put into a landfill?"

"I wonder what happens when a landfill gets full?"

"I wonder how we can dispose of food that is not eaten?"

NOTES

3. Making a Mini-Dump and a Mini-Sanitary Landfill

Explain to the children that they are going to make a mini-dump and a mini-sanitary landfill in the classroom and then compare the two over a long period of time. Invite children to share what they know about dumps and sanitary landfills with the class.

a. You will need the following materials for this experiment:

   two deep, plastic pans

   samples of solid waste, such as apple slices or banana pieces, aluminum foil, cardboard, newspaper strips, glass, plastic bags, steel wool, and fabric pieces

   soil to fill both containers

   sand

   two plastic sheets or bags

b. Have children fill one of the pans half full of soil. Then put each kind of solid waste on top of the soil in the container. Place the container in an area where it will not be disturbed. This container will be the mini-dump.

c. To make the mini-sanitary landfill, have the children place a small amount of soil in the bottom of the second pan. Place a plastic sheet or bag over the soil. Then place each kind of solid waste on top of the plastic in the container. Sprinkle with sand, pat, and then cover with the second sheet of plastic. Cover the plastic with a layer of soil. Pat the soil firmly around the plastic to form a solid seal. This container will be the mini-sanitary landfill. Place the mini-sanitary landfill in an area where it will not be disturbed.

d. From time to time, sprinkle the same amount of water over both the mini-dump and the mini-sanitary landfill. Explain that the sprinkling of water represents natural rainfall.

NOTES

e. After one month, have the children empty the mini-sanitary landfill pan into a big box lined with a plastic bag. Have the children look at the objects to see if they have changed. Also, empty the mini-dump pan into a lined box and see if any changes are occurring there. Encourage children to discuss the changes in each container.

f. Record and date the children's observations on a large chart. Discuss how some items in the mini-dump deteriorate, while others don't. Discuss why the items in the landfill do not deteriorate. Discuss why landfills are sealed (to protect our water supply from leakage of toxic materials—chemicals in batteries, household cleaners, and so on). Discuss the disadvantages of dumps and the possible disadvantages of sanitary landfills.

4. Creating a Compost Pile

Read aloud a selection on the benefits of composting. Then have the children create their own compost pile using the following materials and directions.

a. You will need the following materials:

1 gallon ice-cream container

soil

pencil shavings

food scraps

b. Place a layer of dirt on the bottom of the ice-cream container, then a thin layer of pencil shavings, then a layer of food scraps.

c. Repeat with another layer of dirt, pencil shavings, food scraps, and so on. Keep the dirt moist. Cover the container with a lid.

d. Stir the mixture every two or three days.

e. Every two or three weeks have the children study carefully the deterioration level of the compost. Record and date their observations.

Learning About Air Pollution

The activities in this section focus on how clean the air in the environment is and some of the ways air becomes polluted. In addition to reading aloud to the class a nonfiction selection on air pollution, you will want to provide plenty of opportunities for children to discover information on their own using nonfiction materials.

1. How Clean Is Our Air?

NOTES

Discuss the importance of clean air and why we need clean air to breathe. Explain that the students are going to conduct an experiment to see how clean the air is around their school.

a. Find three sheets of white paper. On two of the sheets, spread solid shortening. Tape one of the shortening-coated papers to the outside of a window and the second shortening-coated paper somewhere in the classroom. Place the third sheet of paper in a drawer where it will stay clean. The next day, compare the three sheets of paper. Discuss the differences among the three sheets. Record the children's observations.

b. Repeat the experiment, but this time expose the shortening-coated papers to the air for an entire week. Then compare the three sheets again. Ask the children to decide how clean the air is that they breathe. Determine if the air inside the classroom is cleaner than the air outside. Record the children's observations, comparing the air inside the classroom with the air outside on a chart entitled "The Air We Breathe" (see page 44).

2. What Makes the Air Dirty?

Explain to the children that they will do an experiment to see what makes the air dirty. You will need two candles, matches, and a glass bottle.

a. First, light one candle and hold it under the glass bottle. Have the children observe what happens. Then light a second candle and hold the glass bottle over the two candles. What happens? Encourage the children to predict what would happen if there were four lighted candles.

b. Have a child rub his or her finger over the blackened glass. Ask the child to describe how the blackened area feels. Encourage children to explain what made the glass black. If they do not know, explain to them what smoke is. Ask the children what they think happens when smoke goes into the air. Discuss various sources of smoke.

THE AIR WE BREATHE			
Date	Paper Without Shortening	Paper Inside with Shortening	Paper Outside with Shortening

c. Have the children locate appropriate nonfiction selections in the school or classroom library on air pollution. If the children can read well enough, ask them to share their books or articles with the class. If the children are beginning readers, ask them to bring the books or articles for you to read aloud to the class.

d. Write facts and other information about air pollution on a large sheet of paper in a web format.

NOTES

3. Counting Cars

During a recess period or a short period before school, have several children count the number of cars that drive by or near the school. Have children count the number of cars that have only one person and the number of cars that have two or more. Have the children report to the class the number of cars in each category. Encourage the children to count the number of times in an evening or a weekend that the family car is used, too. Discuss why we all should try to cut down on car usage.

4. Exploring Ways to Reduce Air Pollution

Ask the children to think about ways we can reduce air pollution. Have them look through the nonfiction materials available in class for suggestions. List the children's suggestions on a large chart.

Recycling Activities

The activities in this section focus on the need for recycling. There are several good fiction books on the theme of recycling, in addition to nonfiction selections you'll want to share with the children. As always, read aloud a nonfiction selection pertaining to this section before beginning an activity.

NOTES

1. Paper Recycling

Explain to the children that the average person in this country throws away about 3.5 pounds of garbage every day. As a class, have students discuss the amounts and types of trash that are thrown into the garbage both at school and at home.

a. Introduce the concept of paper recycling. Explain that paper which is made from previously used paper is called *recycled paper*. Newspapers, napkins, and cardboard are some products that have been made from recycled paper.

b. Share with the class some products made from recycled paper. Ask the children if they can tell any difference between paper that has been recycled and paper that has not. Encourage students to bring to class samples of products that are made of recycled materials. Set up a display of these products in the classroom.

2. Making Recycled Paper

You can make recycled paper in the classroom using the directions from *50 Simple Things Kids Can Do to Save the Earth* by The EarthWorks Group (see the bibliography on page 12).

3. Facts and Information

Ask children to look through several nonfiction selections on paper recycling for facts and important information. Write the children's findings in a web format on a large sheet of butcher paper. Display the web at a level where the children can add new information themselves as the unit progresses.

4. New Uses for Used Items

Bring in a variety of items that can be reused, such as plastic milk jugs, milk cartons, empty pop or soda bottles, aluminum cans, egg cartons, and cardboard tubes. Hold a class meeting to discuss which items can be reused or recycled. Ask the children to explain why recycling is a good thing to do. You might contact your county extension office for information on how to recycle products, too.

5. Take a Recycling Field Trip

Find out if anyone nearby collects or buys newspapers or other items for recycling purposes. Arrange a field trip to the recycling location, if possible.

NOTES

NOTES

6. Recycling Bulletin Board

Use a Venn diagram to show how much trash is actually recyclable.

a. Make a large circle with yarn on one side of a bulletin board. Add the caption "Things We Throw Out" near the circle. Make another circle the same size on the other side of the bulletin board. Have the circles overlap in the middle. Add the caption "Things We Can Reuse" near the second circle.

b. Have the children put pictures of items found in the trash in the appropriate circle. Have them put pictures of reusable items in the other circle. Pictures of recyclable items should go into the center section.

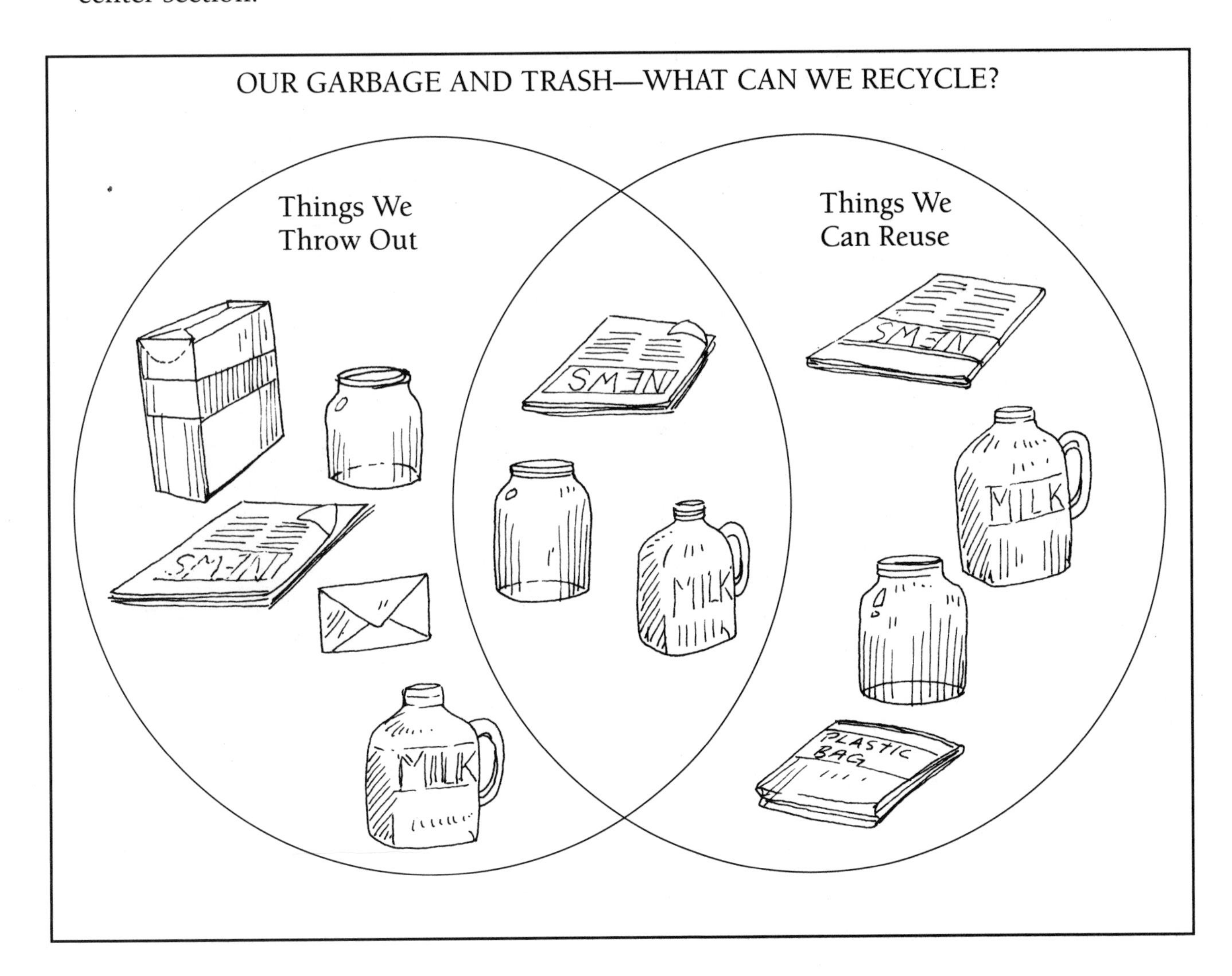

7. Making the World More Beautiful

NOTES

Read the book *Miss Rumphius* by Barbara Cooney aloud to the class. Discuss how Miss Rumphius made the world more beautiful. Ask the children what they can do as a class to help make the world more beautiful, too. List the ideas the children come up with on a large sheet of chart paper. After the ideas are listed, explore with the children ways in which each idea can be accomplished. Then decide on a class project to carry out.

Cross-Curriculum Activities

Writing Arena

Writing helps children think about what they have observed and what they already know. It also helps them synthesize their thoughts and then communicate their ideas to others. Read a nonfiction selection to the class before beginning a writing activity. You might point out some sentences or paragraphs in the selection that are especially well-written.

NOTES

1. Note Writing

If the children have completed Activity 6 on page 34, then, as a large group, write a note to each class explaining how much their trash for one day weighed and what kinds of trash the students found throughout the school. Encourage the children to share with each class what they learned from sorting all the trash for one day in the school.

2. Letter Writing

Have children write letters to other classes in school explaining what they have learned about pollution, recycling, trash, and litter. The letters could contain some tips on what we can all do to help with environmental problems.

3. Writing Big Books About Trash and Litter

Place the children in cooperative working groups. Explain that each group will write and illustrate their own big book on trash and litter.

a. Reread with the children the information they charted about the kinds and amounts of trash and litter collected in and around the school and on their walks.

b. Encourage each group to dictate a story of what they have done, what they have learned, and how they now feel about trash and litter. Write the children's story on chart paper. Skip every other line so that children can make changes later.

c. On another day, reread with each group the draft they dictated. Discuss the changes the children want to make so that the story makes sense and sounds right. Mark any changes necessary directly on the draft.

NOTES

d. Write a final copy. Copy each group's story on large sheets of paper. Leave the top half of the paper blank so the students can illustrate each page. Have the children decide on a title and illustration for the cover. On the title page, list the children in each group as authors.

e. Provide time for children to practice reading what they have written. Make arrangements for them to read their books to children in other classrooms.

4. Writing Little Books

Have each child write a page for a little class book on a topic they've studied in the *Pollution, Recycling, Trash, and Litter* theme unit.

a. *Prewriting.* Hold a class meeting to give the children an opportunity to review and talk about what they have learned about pollution, recycling, trash, and litter.

b. *Drafting.* Encourage students to write a paragraph or dictate to an older student what they have learned about pollution, trash, litter, or recycling and how they feel about it.

c. *Sharing and Revising.* Meet with small groups of three to four students. The purpose of the group is to give children an opportunity to read their drafts to other students to determine if what they have written makes sense and if it sounds right. If students have any suggestions, they should share them with the authors. Authors should try to include the suggestions in their revisions.

d. *Editing.* The children in each group should help each other with spelling and beginning sentences with capitals and ending the sentences with periods. When they are finished, have children make a final copy for the book.

e. *Illustrating.* Encourage students to draw pictures to accompany their writing. Students might draw outline pictures only so that when the book is reproduced, the pictures can be colored by other children.

f. *Publishing.* Put the students' writings and pictures together. Combine all pictures and writings into one class booklet. As a group, decide on a title. List the children's names as authors on the inside cover page. Duplicate the booklet so that each child can have a copy. Give a copy to the principal and place a copy in the media center.

g. *Reading and Sharing Books.* Provide time for the children to read the book and react to each other's writings and drawings. Make arrangements for children to read the book in other classrooms. Encourage the children to take the book home to share with family members, too.

NOTES

Art All Around

Art activities help children visualize the concepts they have been reading about and discussing. Frequently, through art, children will want to review something they have read, heard, or observed so that their artwork is as accurate as they can make it. You'll want to have several resources available for children to refer to. Select a book or magazine article with good photographs or illustrations to read aloud to the class before beginning any activity or activities.

1. Trash Tree Art

Attach a large stick with several branches to the bulletin board. Save the trash from your classroom at the end of the day. Have students tack the trash onto the bulletin board to form a tree. Mark off the number of days on the room calendar that it takes to fill the tree. Encourage children to remove from the tree any pieces of trash they can recycle for other projects.

NOTES

2. Trash Sculpture

Ask children to bring to class clean items they normally would have thrown away—at home or at school. You might ask for materials such as cardboard, Styrofoam, paper scraps, toothpicks, and aluminum foil. Form cooperative working groups of four to five students. Have each group create a sculpture using these materials. Display the sculptures in the cafeteria, media center, and other classrooms, if possible.

3. Milk Carton Birdhouses

Here is a way to recycle milk cartons and help birds, too.

a. You will need a half-gallon milk carton. As an opening for the birds, cut a one-inch hole in the side of the carton approximately two inches from the bottom.

b. Cut a strip from the side of another carton for a perch. Fold the strip and staple it to the milk carton below the hole.

c. Punch two holes in the top of the carton. Thread string through the holes and tie the carton to a tree branch.

Social Studies from Here to There

Children practice being environment-conscious citizens in this section. They use what they have been learning and apply their new knowledge and new attitudes to a situation away from school.

An Earth-Friendly Picnic

NOTES

Ask children how many of them have ever gone on a picnic. Discuss where the children went and what kinds of foods they ate. Discuss, too, what kinds of dishes, tableware, napkins, and containers they had at the picnic. Finally, talk about what is usually thrown away after a picnic is over.

a. Suggest to the children that they have an Earth-friendly picnic. Talk with the children about how they can bring a lunch and have very little garbage. Explore ways they can bring food and something to drink in reusable containers.

b. Send a letter home to parents explaining the purpose of the picnic and asking for their cooperation. A sample letter is provided on page 62 for your convenience.

c. At the end of the picnic, see how much trash is thrown away. Consider composting any food that is not eaten. Have children take turns showing the class their recyclable containers.

Name ______________________________

Trash Survey

Directions: Look through your garbage at home. Put an X by the items that you find. Add any items you find that are not listed.

1.______ newspapers

2.______ aluminum cans

3.______ tin cans

4.______ aluminum foil

5.______ paper towels

6.______ paper grocery bags

7.______ plastic grocery bags

8.______ paper napkins

9.______ other types of paper

10. _____ Styrofoam trays

11.______ disposable diapers

12.______ glass bottles

13.______ plastic bottles

14.______ clear plastic wrap

15.______ egg cartons

16.______ plastic containers

17.______ ______________________

18.______ ______________________

19.______ ______________________

20.______ ______________________

Dear Parent,

During the past several weeks, our class has been studying about pollution in school. We have classified the different items in the trash that are thrown away at school. Will you please help your son or daughter become aware of the types of trash thrown away at home by helping him or her with the enclosed survey? Your child should return the survey to school by ________________________.

We will be talking about ways each of us can help reduce the amount of recyclable items that we throw away—both at home and at school. Please take a few minutes to ask your child about what we are studying in school.

Thank you for your cooperation.

Sincerely,

Dear Parent,

As part of our studies on recycling, we are going to have an Earth-friendly picnic on _____________ at ____________________.

We have talked in school about ways that we can pack a lunch and have very little garbage or trash at the end of our picnic. We have talked about using cloth napkins instead of paper, putting our lunch in reusable containers, using reusable tableware, and bringing a drink in a thermos. Please help your child pack an Earth-friendly lunch for our picnic.

Thank you very much.

Sincerely,

____

is a member of

____

Earth's Friends Club!

Dear Parent,

During the next several weeks, our class will be studying pollution and what we as individuals can do to reduce this very serious problem. As part of our activities, we will be taking several walks around the neighborhoods near our school. One walk will be to look at places that are well-kept and litter free. We will be taking this walking trip on ____________ near _________________________.

Our second trip will be to look for litter and trash. This time we will be picking up all the trash and litter that we see. We plan to take gloves and trash bags along. We will be taking this walk on ________________ in the area of ____________________________.

We need three or four parents to help supervise our walks. If you can join us, please let me know. Thank you!

Sincerely,